Old and New

by Margie Burton, Cathy French, and Tammy Jones

This is a radio.
It is old.

3

This is a radio.

It is new.

This is a car.
It is old.

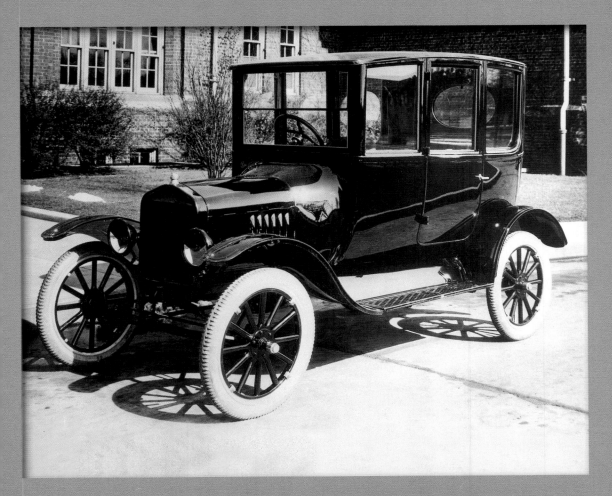

This is a car.

It is new.

This is a train.
It is old.

This is a train.

It is new.

This is a bike.
It is old.

15

Is it old or new?